Hazardous Waste

Look for these and other books in the Lucent Overview
series:

Acid Rain
AIDS
Animal Rights
The Beginning of Writing
Dealing with Death
Drugs and Sports
Drug Trafficking
Endangered Species
Energy Alternatives
Garbage
Hazardous Waste
Homeless Children
Oil Spills
The Olympic Games
Population
Rainforests
Smoking
Soviet-American Relations
Special Effects in the Movies
Teen Alcoholism
The UFO Challenge
Vietnam

Hazardous Waste

by Lila Gano

LUCENT
B·O·O·K·S

LUCENT *Overview Series*   OUR ENDANGERED PLANET

OUR ENDANGERED PLANET

Library of Congress Cataloging-in-Publication Data

Gano, Lila, 1949-
    Hazardous waste / by Lila Gano.
      p.   cm. — (Lucent overview series. Our endangered planet)
    Includes bibliographical references and index.
    Summary: Discusses the scope, legislative angles, and human health
aspects of the hazardous waste problem, as well as future plans for
dealing with hazardous waste.
    ISBN 1-56006-117-0
    1. Hazardous wastes—Juvenile literature.   [1. Hazardous wastes.
2. Refuse and refuse disposal. 3. Pollution.]   I. Title.
II. Series.
TD1030.5.G36   1991
363.72'87—dc20

                         90-23528
                             CIP
                             AC

© Copyright 1991 by Lucent Books, Inc.
P.O. Box 289011, San Diego, CA 92198-0011

Contents

Introduction

NOT LONG AGO, many Americans heard for the first time that hazardous waste threatened their health and the environment. The nation was shocked to discover that toxic, or poisonous, chemicals from this waste were present in water supplies, in people's backyards, and in human bodies. In the worst cases, entire communities had to move because the chemicals polluted everything around them.

What caused this huge environmental problem that affects millions of people? A look at recent history may provide a clue. During World War II, U.S. industry devoted its energies to producing weapons and other war materials. But when the war ended, manufacturers, including the chemical industry, refitted plants to meet the demand for consumer goods in a peacetime economy.

In the laboratory, scientists created new chemicals and materials. More potent chemicals to kill weeds and insects improved agricultural yields. Other new chemicals allowed for the development of plastics, which would be used to create an endless assortment of household products, such as dishes and toys. Better-quality paints, more effective medicines, stronger detergents, and new fabrics like nylon were also developed.

One big chemical company adopted the slogan "better living through chemistry." Consumers

(opposite page) Hazardous waste is frequently treated at incinerators like this one to reduce its toxicity and volume.

7

A local resident points out the many barrels of toxic chemicals stored at this waste site in Nitro, West Virginia.

agreed. Their lives were made easier by advances in chemistry. But these advances came with a price. The new production processes created massive amounts of hazardous waste.

At first, industries large and small sought the easiest and cheapest way to unload the waste produced in their manufacturing operations. This meant dumping it into rivers or oceans, burying it in unlined landfills, or tossing it into garbage dumps. Even the military and the federal government handled their hazardous waste with little concern about the consequences. This uncontrolled dumping, coupled with the absence of laws to monitor hazardous waste, created a major problem that will not be easily solved.

At thousands of sites in the United States, waste threatens people's health and damages the environment. Finding ways to contain or clean up the waste has proven very difficult. When the nation first became aware of the extent of the problem, devising better disposal technologies to burn and bury unwanted waste seemed to be the solution. But, some say, that approach has not worked well.

As communities gained more experience with disposal technologies, one thing became clear. Technology would have some catching up to do. Even today, technology cannot eliminate all hazardous waste. In some cases, it even creates new problems by converting waste from one potentially harmful form to another.

This situation led some researchers and others to support a new concept. These people argue that it makes more sense to stop producing toxic waste than to figure out what to do with it once it exists.

Today, most people agree that hazardous waste presents the world with difficult problems. But they also believe that finding ways to limit the production of hazardous waste and to dispose of it is necessary to ensure a high quality of life on earth.

LOVE CANAL
WE'VE GOT BETTER THINGS TO DO THAN SIT AROUND AND BE CONTAMINATED!!

1

Uncovering a Legacy of Hazardous Waste

BEFORE THE 1970s, few people worried about hazardous waste. As long as the harmful by-products from manufacturing did not affect them, Americans took little notice of how or where they were stored. Laws did not exist to guide hazardous waste disposal. The government did not monitor its trail. Treatment was not required. Research was minimal.

The technological advances that had made the lives of Americans so much easier had also created tons of hazardous waste, and no one really knew what to do with it. The easiest way to get rid of it was to dump it—anywhere.

One of these places where waste was dumped was the town of Love Canal in upstate New York. What happened there turned the nation's attention to the problem of hazardous waste and slipshod disposal practices. A new era of environmental concern and awareness was born when the story of Love Canal hit the news. In this middle-class community, residents discovered a variety of deadly wastes lurking in their backyards.

On the surface, the small community of Love Canal was a typical, suburban neighborhood. Children attended a nearby school, and parents dutifully worked at their jobs to support their families. But residents shared more than just a lifestyle. Their homes and the local school were built near a toxic waste dump that had exposed them to deadly chemicals.

The events leading up to the contamination of an entire community took years to unfold. The story of Love Canal made the headlines in the 1970s, but dumping started in the 1920s. An empty canal in the community became a convenient dump site for waste from a nearby chemical plant and for household trash. In the 1940s, the canal was sold to the Hooker Chemical Company.

The new owners of the canal used it to store

The Hooker Chemical Company dumped tons of toxic wastes at Love Canal. Later, when the site was filled to capacity, the company sold the property to the local school board for one dollar.

more waste. At that time, there were no laws requiring safe disposal methods. Hooker Chemical dug the canal deeper and wider to make more room for its waste, much of which was placed in metal drums and then covered with clay. The clay was expected to keep moisture away from the chemicals and to act as a barrier seal. When the company had filled the site to capacity, it sold the land to the local school board for one dollar.

At the time of the sale, Hooker Chemical told the school board that the site contained chemical waste. Officials at the company must have had an inkling that the chemicals were dangerous because a special clause was added to the deed of sale. The clause stated that Hooker Chemical would not be responsible for any health problems or injuries that might result from using the land.

The school board bought the land anyway and built a school on the edge of the canal. Two roads were built across the canal, and homes soon sprang up on the other side. All the construction activity broke the clay seals that had held the chemicals inside. Several years of heavy rains seeped through the cracks in the clay and corroded the steel drums. The chemicals began to seep out. They traveled through the soil toward the school and hundreds of homes surrounding the canal.

Chemicals on a collision course

Residents living on the edge of the canal did not realize the potential threat creeping toward them. The first sign of trouble at Love Canal occurred in 1958. While building a road, construction workers unearthed cans of leaking chemicals. About the same time, children playing in the dirt near the area experienced chemical burns. Local officials guessed that the leaky drums were the problem. So the drums were reburied, and the problem temporarily put to rest.

A fence surrounds the Love Canal dump site. Families were forced to evacuate the community because of the unsafe chemicals that penetrated their yards, basements, and drinking water.

As time went by, heavy rains and snow caused more of the drums to leak. Residents noticed smelly and discolored soil oozing into their basements. They complained to the New York Health Department and to the federal government. Investigators were surprised at what they finally uncovered in the canal—twenty thousand metric tons of waste in old, rusty barrels. Their findings shocked and surprised the nation.

Hazardous chemicals found

More than four hundred different chemicals were eventually identified at Love Canal. Some of these chemicals were known to cause cancer and birth defects. "Dangerous levels of many toxic chemicals were found in homes bordering the canal, mostly in the basements. Some were measured at 5,000 times the maximum safe concentrations," according to Irene Kiefer, author of *Poisoned Land*. Investigators found not only tainted homes but residents who had absorbed chemicals into their bodies. Though no one can be certain, the serious health problems that plagued the community were probably caused by these chemicals.

Children seemed to experience the worst side effects. Some suffered mysterious illnesses that doctors could not explain. At least one boy is believed to have died of kidney disease linked to dioxin, one of the dangerous chemicals found at Love Canal. The boy's mother, Luella Kenny, said sadly, "He died of playing in his own backyard."

The chemicals at Love Canal also posed a great threat to unborn children. Pregnant women living near the canal experienced very high rates of miscarriage. A miscarriage occurs when an unborn baby is suddenly expelled from its mother's body before it is fully formed and able to survive. And birth defects were more common at Love Canal than in other U.S. communities, studies showed.

Researchers think the miscarriages and birth defects were linked to chromosome damage in the parents caused by exposure to toxic chemicals.

Chromosomes are the genetic material that determines what characteristics people have. In one study of Love Canal residents, one-third of the adults tested showed chromosome damage. Other adults showed evidence of liver damage. The liver is the body's filter system that removes harmful substances from the blood.

The government takes action

After several years of complaints and investigations, the government finally took action to help Love Canal residents. The state of New York purchased more than 230 of their homes and helped residents move. Many of the homes were torn down because harmful chemicals had penetrated

Aerial view of the Love Canal school and community, where residents were exposed to deadly chemicals.

Weeds surround abandoned homes in Love Canal, after hundreds of families relocated to safer communities.

the walls, yards, and water supplies. The federal government declared Love Canal a disaster area, which made residents eligible for government money that they could use to start over. When further studies showed that the contamination had spread, the federal government offered to relocate another 710 families in 1980. Yet for most residents, no amount of money could make up for the loss of their homes or a loved one or calm their fears of what would happen in the future.

Since the disaster, New York state and the federal government have worked hard to clean up Love Canal. More than twelve years and $250 million have been dedicated to containing the toxic waste. During the summer of 1990, the government pronounced one section of Love Canal safe and ready for occupancy. New homes were built and priced low to sell quickly. To keep the harmful chemicals away from residents, the toxic soil was surrounded by a liner of thick clay and then capped off. A chain link fence was placed around the containment site to keep people out. As an added safeguard, the government will monitor the site for leaks.

But some environmental groups are not convinced that Love Canal is safe, despite all these efforts. The Sierra Club, the Natural Resources Defense Council (NRDC), and others have threatened legal action against the government in order

Two residents vacate the chemically contaminated Love Canal community. After several years of complaints and investigations, the federal government took action to help Love Canal residents relocate.

to prevent the sale of these new homes. "I'd like to see a lot more information on the health risks before making a major policy decision to move people back," said Rebecca Todd, a lawyer for the NRDC.

Because the new homes at Love Canal are inexpensive, young families are interested in buying them. Could the tragedy of Love Canal repeat itself with these new residents? Some families are willing to take that chance.

Lessons from Love Canal

Americans learned some tough lessons from the events at Love Canal. That community was only one of thousands of toxic waste sites littering the country. Some experts estimate that from thirty to fifty thousand sites exist, many yet undiscovered. Even today, contaminated communities are still

Joel Pett/*The Lexington Herald-Leader.* Reprinted with permission.

making headlines and fighting corporate polluters. In 1990, an oil refinery bought out a small town devastated by oil leaks that saturated the soil. The company bought four hundred homes for eighteen million dollars but never admitted responsibility for the leaks. Like Love Canal, most residents left to start new lives.

The federal government declared Love Canal a disaster area in the late 1970s.

Love Canal also made the public aware of the lack of regulations controlling hazardous waste disposal. Dumping toxic waste into rivers and other places was for the most part legal before Love Canal. Even large, respected companies that could have afforded to treat and contain their toxic waste went along with the common practice of carelessly dumping it. Legislation passed in the 1980s has made such dumping illegal. Yet illegal dumping continues. Critics charge that the government has been ineffective in handling the country's waste problem despite good intentions. One reason may be the overwhelming size of the problem.

2

How Big Is the Problem?

HARDLY A DAY goes by that a story about hazardous waste does not appear in a newspaper somewhere in the United States. So vast is the problem that the Environmental Protection Agency (EPA), which monitors the waste, describes the problem as "almost impossible to comprehend."

Each year, the problem seems to get worse. More people discover that they are living near or on top of lots that were once hazardous waste dump sites. When stories about Love Canal and other contaminated communities first surfaced, basic questions needed answers—what is hazardous waste, how much is out there, and where did it come from? These questions are still being asked today.

Coming up with a definition

Just what is a hazardous waste? Because countless chemicals have the capacity to be toxic under the right circumstances, coming up with an exact definition was not easy. The government talked to scientists, citizens, and people in industry before deciding that, simply put, hazardous waste is any waste, garbage, or refuse material that may cause

(opposite page) Suited in protective gear, federal technicians gather soil samples which they suspect are contaminated with dioxin.

or contribute to illness, death, or environmental damage. The waste can be liquid, solid, semisolid, or a gas or vapor.

Under this definition, hundreds of substances qualify as hazardous waste. In Louisiana, a toxic vapor from a harmful liquid waste poisoned cows. The chemical hexachlorobenzene (HCB) was dumped in a landfill near cow pastures. The liquid HCB evaporated into the air and created a toxic vapor that poisoned cattle up to one hundred miles away.

HCB is just one of approximately 450 substances that the government has identified as hazardous. Researchers constantly study suspicious substances to decide if they are harmful. As new information becomes available, the EPA revises its list. This list includes numerous substances used daily by all kinds of businesses and industries. Eventually, these substances end up in the waste materials business and industry produce.

How much waste is out there?

Measuring the amount of hazardous waste produced is a difficult task. Nevertheless, the EPA estimated that U.S. industry generated 275 million tons of hazardous waste in 1985. That was more than one ton per person, or enough to fill the New Orleans Superdome fifteen hundred times.

More recent estimates reveal a disturbing trend. Despite efforts to control and reduce waste production, we are creating more, not less. By 1989, the yearly production rate was between 500 and 600 million tons. If these figures are accurate, the United States produces ten times more hazardous waste than any other nation.

But getting a clear picture of how much toxic waste is produced is not easy. Companies and the military are required to file periodic reports with the government detailing the amount of waste

A worker measures the toxicity of waste leaking from a petroleum drum. Of the 1.5 billion undergound drums that contain hazardous wastes, the EPA estimates one-fourth are leaking.

they generate. But governmental reporting regulations are often hard to understand and change frequently.

Another factor complicates measuring the volume of toxic waste. The government relies on the companies that generate the waste to complete these reports. That means those companies also decide which substances to report. Proper hazardous waste disposal can be complex and expensive. Although many companies honestly and accurately report the amount and types of waste they produce, others are not as careful. Some even falsify their records. For these reasons, it is sometimes difficult to monitor the sources of hazardous waste.

"THE TOXIC WASTE DUMP MEANS A LOT OF JOBS FOR THE AREA... DOCTORS, NURSES, HEALTH THERAPISTS..."

Although hazardous waste comes in many forms, most of it is generated by a handful of industries. Those industries include manufacturers of chemicals, petroleum products, plastics, metals, and transportation and electrical equipment. Together, they create more than 90 percent of the toxic waste in the United States. More than forty thousand companies within these industries produce at least two thousand pounds of hazardous waste each month. The U.S. military and its contractors are also major producers of toxic waste. Much of their waste comes from making weapons and other equipment. But hazardous waste is found closer to home, too.

Neighborhood businesses are also a source of toxic waste. Automotive repair shops, laundromats, dry cleaners, construction companies, and photo processing centers generate toxic wastes. More than half of the hazardous waste created by small companies comes from old vehicle batteries collected by auto repair shops. Batteries contain harmful lead and acids that have become a hazardous waste problem in most industrialized nations. Dry cleaning chemicals and leftover chemicals from printing and developing photos are also toxic waste.

Hazardous waste also comes from many of the products Americans use around their homes. Typical household hazardous waste includes used motor oil, cleaners that contain acids, pesticides, and paints. When these products reach garbage landfills, they can cause explosions and fires or filter into water supplies beneath the soil.

Whether in large or small amounts, hazardous

Every year, this manufacturing plant in Texas produces more than 200 million tons of ethylene glycol, a chemical used to make synthetic fibers and antifreeze. Such chemical manufacturers generate a large portion of the hazardous waste produced in the U.S.

Discarded batteries may leak harmful lead and acids into the ground. Here, Congressman Brian Bosma informs Indiana residents of the state's new battery recycling law. The law states that retailers must accept used batteries for recycling in exchange for new batteries purchased.

waste has to go somewhere. Before the strict laws of the 1980s were passed, companies dumped untreated waste into rivers, along country roads, or in landfills meant for household trash. These disposal methods were the cheapest and fastest way to handle the waste. Most companies were not concerned and much of the public was unaware of the impact of these practices on the nation's health.

Careless dumping and disposal practices created thousands of hazardous waste sites all over the country. Some experts believe that between ten and fifty thousand sites exist. Because there are so many, the federal government decided to tackle the most serious ones first. The EPA created a special list of sites that posed the greatest threat to the environment and the public. The sites on this list are commonly referred to as the Superfund sites. This list is called the National Priorities List (NPL). There were 1,218 sites on this list in early 1989, and the number keeps growing.

The federal government and state agencies have spent billions of dollars trying to clean up these sites. Yet by the summer of 1990, only fifty had been cleaned or contained so that they no longer posed a threat. Why has so little progress been made? The job was much bigger than first believed. "There are far more sites that are far more difficult to deal with than anybody anticipated," explained former EPA director Lee Thomas.

Where are these Superfund sites? They exist in every state and even in the U.S. territory of Guam. New Jersey tops the list with 109 sites and proposed sites. Pennsylvania is in second place with 96, followed by California with 91. The tropical island of Oahu in Hawaii has 6 sites. These sites in Hawaii were created when pineapple pesticides were dumped on the ground. The chemicals seeped into groundwater and tainted several drinking wells.

The cost of cleaning up hazardous waste is very high. The bill for the Superfund sites alone is expected to run to more than $23 billion. Cleanup costs for the thousands of remaining sites will certainly top $100 billion. But if we do not clean them up, the results may be far more costly. The health and welfare of this generation and those to come are at stake.

Why is hazardous waste a problem?

Disposal of dangerous waste is a major environmental problem because, slowly but surely, much of the waste finds its way into drinking water, the soil, and the air. When enough toxic chemicals enter the human body, illness and death can result. Environmentalist Barry Commoner puts it this way: "We are poisoning ourselves and our prosperity."

One key to our prosperity and survival is an abundant supply of drinking water. But toxic waste has threatened groundwater, which is a major source of drinking water. About half the nation depends on groundwater. Toxic waste and leaking gasoline drums have polluted much of

Before the stricter laws of the 1980s, homes and industries disposed of untreated waste into landfills meant for trash, along country roads, or into rivers, such as the Patroon Creek in New York.

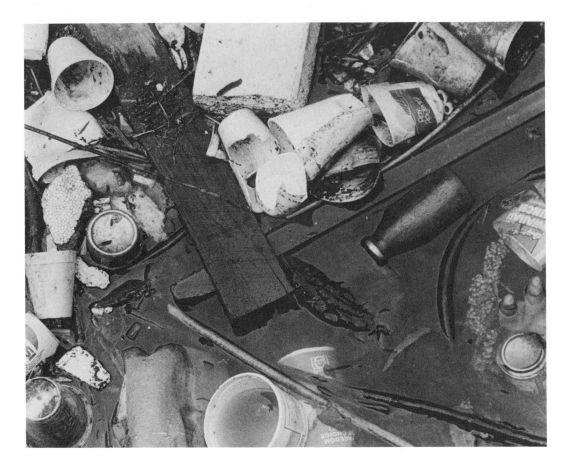

Waste and debris wash to the surface of a landfill after a heavy rainfall. Such poorly contained landfills threaten drinking water, air, and soil.

this valuable resource.

Poorly constructed landfills that contain hazardous waste are a prime source of groundwater contamination. As rains or other liquids enter the landfills, they mix with toxic chemicals. This mixture of pollutants and liquid is called leachate. The leachate slowly seeps deeper into the soil and poisons groundwater. Once groundwater has been contaminated, it is very hard to restore its original purity.

Leaking gasoline drums at service stations pose another threat to water supplies. There are roughly 1.5 million underground drums containing petroleum products or other hazardous substances. The EPA estimates that one-fourth are leaking or soon will. Countless towns and cities have already struggled with this problem.

When the Massachusetts community of Truro detected gasoline in its drinking water, residents took legal action. The court sided with them and forced the company responsible to pay for bottled water. The company was also ordered to clean up the water supply, a task that cost millions of dollars.

Toxic waste in one form or another has infiltrated communities all over the country. Love Canal was among the first to feel the results of years of careless dumping. There will probably be other Love Canals in other places, and many Americans worry that something similar could happen to them.

3

The Health Risks of Hazardous Waste

HARMFUL CHEMICALS FROM hazardous waste can enter the body in several ways. The simple act of breathing may bring toxic vapors into the lungs and bloodstream. Toxic substances can also enter the body through the skin. Contaminated food, milk, or water also bring harmful substances into the body. When carelessly released into the environment or animal food supplies, harmful substances can easily become part of the human food chain.

The body is equipped to handle some unhealthy substances. It often rids itself of undesirable substances as blood is filtered through the liver. Substances are also excreted in bodily wastes. But many chemicals found in hazardous waste are not expelled from the body. Instead, they accumulate in fat cells and remain there indefinitely. For this reason, waste materials containing certain hazardous substances are especially troubling.

Dioxin, a general term for a class of seventy-five chlorine-related compounds, is one of the most toxic substances known. It earned this reputation

(opposite page) A sign warns residents to stay out of contaminated water. Toxic chemicals can penetrate the body through the skin.

31

when hundreds of pounds of dioxin waste were uncovered at Love Canal. The dioxin debate heated up even more when one scientist said that it is so potent that only a few ounces are enough to kill everyone in New York City. Dioxin never really posed a threat to New York, but in 1983 a small town in Missouri was ruined by the deadly chemical.

In Times Beach, Missouri, a toxic mix-up ultimately forced twenty-four hundred residents to move. As in many towns in Missouri, in Times Beach it was a common practice to occasionally spray the ground to keep the dust down. The ground was sprayed with waste oil from service stations and chemical factories. Russell Bliss earned his living collecting the waste oils and spraying them throughout towns in Missouri. He

Local citizens encourage Times Beach residents to apply for aid after dioxin was detected in the soil in 1983.

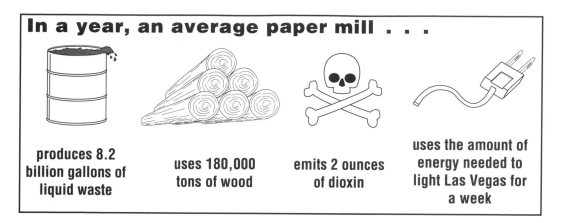

In a year, an average paper mill . . .

produces 8.2 billion gallons of liquid waste

uses 180,000 tons of wood

emits 2 ounces of dioxin

uses the amount of energy needed to light Las Vegas for a week

spread the oil over parking lots, horse stables, streets, and farms. Bliss did not realize that dioxin from a factory that produced weed killers was mixed in with much of the oil.

Shortly after spraying one area of Times Beach, animals started dying and a child became very sick. When health officials investigated, they discovered dioxin in the soil at the location where the problems had occurred. The contaminated soil was removed on two separate occasions, and everyone thought the threat was over. But they were wrong.

Dioxin remained in the soil at very high levels. And when a nearby river flooded, dioxin spread to other areas of the town. There was so much dioxin in Times Beach that the government began to worry about the health of residents. To prevent everyone from getting sick, the state and federal government bought—and closed off—the entire town. They also helped people move and start over again.

What happened in Times Beach was not a freak accident. Dozens of similarly contaminated towns exist in Missouri and in other states. Yet scientists could not agree then, and still do not agree today, on how much dioxin presents a health hazard. This leaves people wondering and worrying about how much is really safe.

A worker oversees the papermaking process. When the paper is bleached, dioxin forms as a waste by-product. Modern mills use scrubbers to remove much of this dioxin.

Throughout northwestern Florida, paper mills are a common sight. In the papermaking process, dioxin is a waste by-product formed when paper is bleached. Modern mills have scrubbers and other equipment to remove much of the dioxin from the waste. But it is not uncommon for small amounts to be discharged in waste that enters waterways.

Some paper mills have released too much dioxin into nearby waters, according to Florida health officials. Fish absorb the chemical and pass it on to humans when the tainted fish is eaten. Health officials worry that over a period of time, people who eat a lot of fish laced with dioxin will get sick.

Most scientists agree that dioxin in sufficient doses is deadly and can cause cancer, skin problems, liver damage, and other illnesses. But they disagree on what levels can be safely ingested by humans or tolerated in the environment. Even

Fish may absorb the dioxin flushed into waterways by local paper mills. Health officials worry that the toxins will be passed on to humans.

agencies within the federal government disagree on safe dioxin levels. The EPA has established seven parts per trillion as a warning level. This means that in a sample of water or soil or some other substance containing one trillion molecules, no more than seven of them should be dioxin molecules. The Food and Drug Administration (FDA), the government agency responsible for ensuring that our food and medicines do not harm us, believes that nearly four times that amount is acceptable in food.

Food is our primary source of dioxin, according to the Centers for Disease Control in Atlanta, Georgia, and most dioxin in our diet comes from beef. This occurs when cattle eat grass sprayed with weed killers made with dioxin. The dioxin remains in their tissues.

One of the most hazardous members of the dioxin family, TCDD, commonly enters the body in this way. But this substance, which has been found in at least twenty-eight Superfund sites, can also enter the body in other ways. Children playing in contaminated soil can absorb TCDD through their skin. People who live near city or industrial incinerators where TCDD wastes are burned may breathe small amounts that linger in ashes in the air.

Polychlorinated biphenyls (PCBs)

Other chemicals that threaten human health and the environment include polychlorinated biphenyls (PCBs). PCBs are a family of heat-resistant liquid chemicals introduced in the 1930s. Because of their ability to withstand high heat, PCBs have been used as coolants in electrical equipment, such as transformers, television sets, and motors. They have also been used to make paints, adhesives, plastics, and printing ink. In spite of the variety of practical uses, PCBs had a

When cattle eat grass sprayed with weed killers that contain dioxin, the chemical remains in their tissues. The toxic substance is then passed on to humans in the form of tainted beef.

major drawback. They were perhaps the most poisonous substances ever produced.

Medical studies show that PCBs can cause a host of illnesses. "There is evidence that PCBs can cause cancer, birth defects, and damage to skin, eyes, and lungs," according to science book author Malcolm Weiss.

Recognizing the harm that PCBs could do, some nations banned their production. Western Europe and Japan no longer make PCBs. The United States banned their production in 1979. But the government may have acted too late. Writer Stephen Zipko explains why in his book, *Toxic Threat*: "About 1.4 billion pounds of PCBs have been made in North America. Of this amount, 450 million pounds are now in the environment. Another 750 million pounds are still in use, and some of them will slowly enter the environment because PCBs are persistent. . . . Wherever old electrical equipment is dumped, it may leak PCBs into the water."

Despite such warnings, PCB levels—which seriously threatened human health and the environment—have declined because of the ban. Unfortunately, other nations continue to make PCBs, mainly because industries have pressed these governments into allowing them to produce and sell the chemicals for profit.

Mercury

Humans have had a very long association with the naturally occurring metal called mercury, which is poisonous. Samples of mercury have been found in Egyptian tombs dating back to 1500 B.C. Because it looks like flowing silver, ancient people believed mercury was magic.

As scientists discredited these magic properties, practical purposes were found for mercury. For a long time, it was used to treat animal furs so they could be made into hats. Hatmakers, or hatters, breathed the toxic mercury vapors over long peri-

ods, and this sometimes caused them to suffer slight brain damage. This led to unusual behavior, such as emotional outbursts and uncontrollable shaking. The expression "mad as a hatter" probably evolved because of the bizarre behaviors caused by mercury poisoning.

In more recent times, an entire community was poisoned by mercury waste in its food supply. The incident occurred in the village of Minamata on an island off the coast of Japan in 1956. A local plastics plant was using mercury to speed its production process. Once the work was done, the mercury was discarded.

Rather than store or treat the mercury waste, plant workers dumped it into the bay. This act set off a chain of events that led to the deaths of more than fifty Minamata residents. When mercury entered the seawater, a chemical reaction occurred that made it even more poisonous. The fish and shellfish absorbed the toxic metal, and the villagers and their pets ate the seafood. The villagers did not realize an important food source had been poisoned.

First, the village cats became ill from the contaminated seafood. Their movements were uncoordinated, and their behavior became unpredictable. Many villagers soon displayed similar symptoms. As their muscles weakened, some trembled and behaved oddly. The mercury affected their memory and their ability to hear, taste, see, and smell. Some of these symptoms later appeared in the children of women who had eaten the seafood while they were pregnant.

Who was responsible?

The toxic tragedy at Minamata was clearly caused by exposure to the mercury waste that was dumped by the plastics manufacturer. But many years passed before the company admitted its mistake. By then, about four hundred tons of mercury had been dumped into the bay, and people in other areas of the island were becoming ill.

The Japanese are not the only ones who have handled mercury carelessly. In the United States, countless companies have dumped mercury waste in waterways and landfills all over the country. The EPA has identified 175 toxic waste sites that contain mercury and has placed them on the Na-

In this Japanese fishing village near Minamata, local residents were poisoned when they ate fish contaminated by mercury.

tional Priorities List.

Each person reacts differently to toxic substances. Some may show signs of illness while others do not. The pattern of illness and health problems at Love Canal is one example of how hard it is to predict health risks.

Not all children at Love Canal got sick. Nor did all adults suffer chromosome damage. Yet enough were ill or had physical problems to convince officials that something was very wrong there. For those who left Love Canal, their bodies may get rid of some of the toxins. But some substances will remain in fat tissue for years. Harmful side effects may not surface for decades. If former res-

Love Canal children hold up homemade signs urging the government to provide money to help families relocate.

idents develop unusual health problems later in life, doctors may suspect that exposure to the chemicals at Love Canal is to blame. But proving that theory will not be easy.

Another factor complicates the study of health risks and toxic waste. Identifying the source of the waste is often difficult. Intense investigative work by the victims and their families, government officials, and medical and lab specialists is required. Often, it takes several years to prove a case and force the responsible parties to correct the problem. By then, more people have become ill.

For these reasons, the study of toxic substances has been called an inexact science. Conflicting opinions have created questions, delayed corrective actions, and fueled many arguments. Though at times chaotic, the continuing debate over toxic waste has also prompted the passage of many laws designed to protect human health and the environment.

4

Hazardous Waste and the Law

As EARLY AS the 1960s, Americans realized they were poorly prepared to handle the growing volume of trash and solid waste they produced. Each year, households across the country threw away tons of grass clippings, newspapers, and food wrappers. Restaurants discarded mountains of used paper products, plastic, and tin cans. Even cities and towns generated solid waste in the form of chipped concrete, paper, and boards from construction projects, for example. Faced with increasing amounts of refuse and fewer places to put it, the nation turned to Congress to help solve the problem.

In 1965, Congress passed the Solid Waste Disposal Act. This was the first federal law to encourage cities, businesses, and households to improve solid waste disposal methods. The law targeted household garbage, commercial refuse, sludge, and other materials produced by industry. Unfortunately, the Solid Waste Disposal Act focused primarily on nonhazardous waste.

The average citizen did not realize that it was a common industrial practice to deposit hazardous waste in unlined, open pits. These treatment pits, or lagoons, allowed toxic substances to evaporate

43

into the air or seep into groundwater. Toxic substances were sometimes sealed in drums and delivered to city or county landfills. Leaking drums posed a threat to underground water supplies and were fire hazards. As Americans became better informed about toxic waste, they demanded that their government take action to protect them and the environment.

The first big step

In 1976, Congress finally acted. It amended the Solid Waste Disposal Act by including hazardous waste. This amendment was called the Resource Conservation and Recovery Act (RCRA). RCRA was designed with several goals in mind: protecting human health and the environment from hazardous waste, conserving energy and natural resources, reducing the amount of all types of waste, and ensuring that hazardous waste was managed in an "environmentally sound manner."

Under the RCRA, an "environmentally sound manner" meant closely tracking hazardous waste. Most hazardous waste is produced by large companies that treat, store, and dispose of it on-site.

Ed Gamble. Reprinted with permission.

Smaller companies, however, often transported their waste to other locations for disposal. During transport, roadside dumping often was the quickest and cheapest way to get rid of the waste.

Roadside dumping became much more difficult to get away with under the RCRA. The new law set up a complex tracking system to monitor the delivery and arrival of hazardous waste to authorized storage and treatment facilities. Today, waste is still tracked from the time it is generated at the industrial site until it is disposed of legally. This system is sometimes referred to as the "cradle-to-grave" approach. Its success has been mixed. Although many companies have tried to comply with this process, others have found ways around the law.

The land ban

An unsettling discovery in 1984 refocused the nation's attention on hazardous waste disposal. Engineers and scientists found that the EPA-accepted method of containing most waste was flawed. Roughly 80 percent of all hazardous waste was disposed of by burying it inside the earth. Despite special linings and barriers to prevent the waste from seeping, leaks occurred after several years. These leaks threatened the water supplies of communities and wildlife habitats.

Specially lined landfills, underground steel- or concrete-lined shafts called injection wells, and man-made ponds called surface impoundments were the primary methods used to bury contaminated waste.

Looking for a more permanent solution, Congress was forced to rethink earlier approaches. In 1984, Congress amended the RCRA and called for important changes in land disposal techniques. The amended law banned unsafe and untreated waste from land disposal and tightened construction standards on land disposal facilities in an effort to prevent leaks. Congress also directed the EPA to phase out the practice of disposing hazardous waste in landfills unless the waste was previously treated.

Under this "land ban," waste must first undergo treatment by the best available technology to reduce its toxicity. In most cases, that means incineration, or burning, at extremely high temperatures. This process reduces not only the toxicity but also the volume of waste. Because space for landfills is limited, reducing the volume of waste is also important.

The RCRA amendment did more than restrict the use of land as a method of waste containment. The law also ordered a new approach to hazardous waste management. It determined that the best way to manage hazardous waste was not to

In this 1975 photo, chemical waste covers the ground at a dumping site in Iowa. Congress has since tightened the standards for disposing of hazardous waste.

create it in the first place. This approach is called waste minimization.

Under the law, waste generators are required to tell the EPA what they are doing to decrease waste production. Generators must certify that they have taken steps to reduce their volume and must report on the progress they have achieved. Often, an engineer has to redesign a company's manufacturing process, which can be expensive at first. In the long run, however, the company will have to pay less for waste disposal services, and the public and environment will benefit by less exposure to toxic substances or residues from the disposal process.

Cleaning up the mistakes of the past

There seemed to be an epidemic of abandoned, leaking hazardous waste sites during the late 1970s and early 1980s. The RCRA legislation was designed to prevent future incidents, but how were the mistakes of the past to be corrected?

Pushed by angry citizens and activists, Congress once again responded after the damage had been done. In 1980, Congress enacted the Comprehensive Environmental Response, Compensation, and Liability Act (CERCLA). The provisions of CERCLA were designed to remedy past mistakes. The act ordered the government to identify places where releases of hazardous waste had already occurred or might occur. It also required the government to remedy the damage caused by these releases and to try to get the people or companies responsible for the releases to pay for the cleanup.

This act also created the Superfund account, which was established to pay for corrective action. Its money was to come from taxes on oil and some chemical products.

But by 1986, Congress realized that cleaning up hazardous waste sites was going to take more

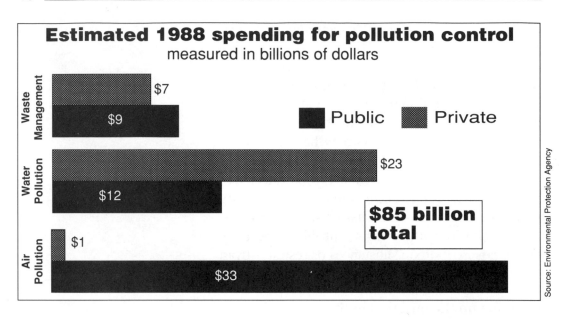

Estimated 1988 spending for pollution control
measured in billions of dollars

Waste Management
$7
$9

Public   Private

Water Pollution
$23
$12

$85 billion total

Air Pollution
$1
$33

Source: Environmental Protection Agency

money and time. The vast number of hazardous waste sites and the expense of cleanup was far more than most people had imagined. Few sites had been cleaned up after five years of spending, planning, and filing lawsuits against responsible parties. Managing the cleanups had become difficult because everyone was learning as they went along.

In 1986, more money was pumped into the Superfund, increasing the total to $8.5 billion. The amendment to increase funding was called the Superfund Amendments and Reauthorization Act of 1986 (SARA). Based on the experiences of past cleanup efforts, SARA also set up a schedule for cleaning up sites on the National Priorities List.

Sites are chosen for this list by a complex formula known as the Hazard Ranking System. This system is a mathematical model that determines the risk to the public and the environment posed by hazardous substances at a site. Points are awarded to a site based on what chemicals it contains and how close the site is to communities, water sources, and wildlife habitats.

Under SARA, more funding was provided to study toxic substances. Descriptions, sometimes called profiles, of toxic substances commonly found at waste sites were prepared. These profiles contain general information about the medical effects of the various toxins, what levels are considered harmful, and a review of related research.

Despite the money and effort expended through the Superfund program, the results are disappointing. Critics of the Superfund say that it has moved too slowly. Only a handful of sites have been cleaned up since the program began a decade ago. Others complain that the EPA spends more money studying the sites and searching for the responsible parties than cleaning them up.

Shifting the burden to the states

Initially, the federal government led the fight to control and clean up toxic waste. As more knowledge and experience emerged, however, the federal government has turned over much of the responsibility to the states, which have, over the years, taken a more active role. As the hazardous waste problem continues to grow, the federal government cannot supply all the required money and effort. Many thousands of hazardous waste sites need attention, yet only the worst are designated for cleanup with federal Superfund dollars. If the problems at these less toxic sites are to be corrected, state governments must take charge, federal officials have said.

As a result, more than forty states plus Guam and the District of Columbia have been authorized by the EPA to run their own hazardous waste programs. Once a state proves that its program is as strict as the EPA's, the EPA grants it permission to operate. Today, most states manage their own programs with some enforcement assistance from the EPA.

EPA technicians check soil for dioxin contamination during the Times Beach crisis.

Increasingly, citizen groups are taking the initiative to protect their environment. Here, workers gather debris to test it for toxicity before it may be transported to a landfill in Wright City, Missouri. Residents living near the landfill obtained a temporary restraining order halting its transportation.

Enforcement should become easier as state governments write their own regulations. Many states have already enacted laws that mirror the contents of CERCLA or the RCRA. Twenty states use a priority list similar to the NPL. Two states have led the way in requiring industry to minimize wastes. These states, Massachusetts and Oregon, have passed laws forcing industry to reduce the amount of hazardous waste produced. Other states are considering similar legislation.

With the memories of Love Canal lingering in the minds of state legislators, some states have sought to protect victims of hazardous waste releases. Eleven states have laws that require offenders to compensate victims for relocation expenses or for obtaining clean water when water supplies are tainted.

Lawmakers in some states have also taken steps to protect unsuspecting buyers from purchasing contaminated real estate. Sellers of certain types of commercial property, such as the site of a paint factory, must provide information about the storage, disposal, or release of hazardous waste on the property. If the site is contaminated, the state may hold up the sale or require that it be cleaned up.

Regulating hazardous waste has created a complex set of laws at both the state and federal level. As new information comes to light about disposal methods, waste reduction techniques, and the health effects of hazardous substances, the laws will be revised and updated. While companies push to preserve their right to do business, citizen groups push for their right to a safe environment. With high stakes on both sides, these groups struggle to influence the legislative process.

5

The Problem of Nuclear Waste

THE POWER OF nuclear energy was harnessed about fifty years ago by scientists exploring the mysteries of the atom. At the time, this research seemed destined for only one purpose: building powerful nuclear weapons.

But as research continued, scientists found other uses for nuclear power. Today, nuclear energy produces electricity and plays an important part in advancing medical technology as well as weaponry. What science still has not discovered, however, is a completely safe method for storing or disposing of the hazardous waste that nuclear energy produces.

This waste differs from other hazardous waste in one important respect. In varying degrees, it is radioactive. This means the waste has undergone atomic changes causing it to give off potentially harmful energy.

Although some radioactive materials decay to a harmless state within hours, others remain dangerous for thousands of years. Plutonium, a radioactive material used in advanced weapons, takes twenty-four thousand years to lose just half of its potency, or strength. It is so dangerous that technicians who work with plutonium must not

(opposite page) Science has yet to uncover a safe method for storing nuclear waste. Pictured here is the Three Mile Island Nuclear Plant in Pennsylvania.

even allow it to touch their skin since it can cause cancer and death.

In general, radiation exposure can damage cells inside the body. Cell damage can range from slight to severe, depending on the length of exposure and the potency of the radioactive material. If cells are severely damaged, leukemia, bone cancer, lung cancer, and other types of serious illness may result. If reproductive cells are harmed, offspring may have birth defects. The harm caused by too much radiation sometimes takes decades to show up, and not everyone exposed to

Wearing protective gear, workers bury potentially dangerous containers of radioactive materials at the Idaho National Engineering Laboratory.

the same dose will become ill. These inconsistencies have sparked many questions about what levels of exposure are safe.

How much is too much?

Because people react differently to radiation, scientists are still asking, "How much is too much?" Dr. John Gofman, a nuclear physics pioneer, believes that there are no safe doses of exposure. Even very low doses can be harmful and cause cancer, he concluded from his research. Others believe that the body can tolerate small doses of radiation and that workers can safely do their jobs around nuclear waste, if they are shielded from harmful materials.

Because some nuclear materials pose a health threat, what to do with this contaminated waste raises many questions and concerns. Scientists have been unable to say with certainty just how long nuclear waste can be safely stored, for example. Likewise, scientists have been unable to agree on the best locations and methods for storing or disposing of this waste. Some scientists think nuclear waste can be recycled. Others are not so sure. So many unanswered questions make only one thing clear: a great deal of scientific work lies ahead.

Uranium mining

The nuclear age has left behind a trail of nuclear waste. The trail begins at the uranium mines located in the western United States. There tons of uranium are mined and milled for use in nuclear reactors. The milling process separates the uranium from the rock that surrounds it but leaves behind a grayish sand called tailings. The tailings are radioactive and collect in piles near the mines.

Care must be taken to keep the radioactive tailings away from humans and animals, their food, and water supplies. This is because harmful radiation can seep into groundwater or wash into pastures, contaminating cattle and the milk and meat they provide.

Despite this threat, people have not been careful in storing or disposing of uranium tailings. In the past, the tailings were left out in the open to be carried away by the winds and the rain. Stephen Zipko explains what happened at mines in Colorado: "Twelve million tons of radioactive tailings are stacked at eleven sites on the banks of the Colorado River and its tributaries. An estimated 3 million tons of these tailings have blown away or washed into the river. This river system supplies Phoenix, Los Angeles, and much of the Southwest with irrigation and drinking water."

Radiation exposure in Colorado

In Grand Junction, Colorado, in the 1960s, thousands of people were exposed to radiation from uranium tailings. At that time, the government allowed builders to use the tailings for making concrete, which was used to fill in holes around construction projects. The concrete was poured in driveways and around swimming pools and sewer lines. But the most serious threat came from tailings used in the foundations of homes and offices.

By the early 1970s, the government realized that the radioactive tailings should not have been used in construction projects. At a cost of more than twelve million dollars, the government replaced the foundations of buildings all over Grand Junction. Because of the problems there, the government passed a law in 1978 requiring tailings to be contained and prevented from entering the environment.

Today, only a few uranium mines are in operation. Nonetheless, problems, including tainted

groundwater at storage sites, still exist. Attention has shifted in recent years, however, to other nuclear waste concerns.

Over 110 nuclear power plants supply about 20 percent of this nation's electricity. Worldwide, more than 400 nuclear power plants exist in twenty-five countries. The main advantage of nuclear power is that it does not pollute the air. Conventional power plants burn fossil fuels like oil, coal, and gas and cause major air pollution problems.

Steel drums containing low-level nuclear waste are dumped into a trench at a waste disposal facility in Illinois.

Waste from nuclear power plants

When nuclear power plants were being built, however, little attention was given to the waste these nuclear plants produced. This waste falls into two categories—low-level and high-level.

Low-level waste consists of rags soiled from cleaning radioactive equipment, gloves, clothing, or tools exposed to radiation. Low-level waste is generally not as harmful as high-level waste and decays quicker. Nevertheless, low-level waste must still be handled with caution. This type of waste is stored in special containers and buried in trenches. The trenches are covered with layers of sand, compacted clay, gravel and stone, and topsoil. The high-level waste from nuclear power plants presents a more difficult problem. It has no place to go.

High-level radioactive waste consists mostly of spent pellets and fuel rods used for powering nuclear reactors. About twenty-four million pounds of high-level waste are temporarily stored in large pools of water in vaults at the plants while scientists search for more permanent solutions.

An aerial view of a solid waste storage area in Oak Ridge, Tennessee. The waste area was used for shallow land burial of low-level radioactive waste. Low-level waste is easier to store than high-level waste because it decays more quickly.

It is unlikely that more nuclear power plants will be built soon. Yet waste from existing ones continues to pile up. By the year 2000, about forty-three thousand metric tons of used fuel will have collected, researchers estimate. Although many scientists say this waste should be stored deep underground, the solution remains in dispute.

Also in dispute is what to do with the nuclear plants themselves when they grow old and are no longer efficient or useful. Because many of the inner workings of a nuclear power plant are radioactive, and will remain so for many years, the plants themselves could become a serious form of hazardous waste.

A typical modern nuclear plant, being dismantled after thirty years of operation, would amount to about eighteen thousand cubic yards of contaminated concrete and steel, two researchers with Energy System Research Group in Boston wrote in 1989. Researchers Bruce Biewald and Donald Marron contend that the remains of such a plant would contain about five million curies, a measure of the amount of radioactivity emitted. By way of comparison, the two researchers note that the largest nuclear plant to be dismantled in the United States, the Elk River Reactor, contained about ten thousand curies of radioactivity when it was closed after only four years of operation.

Nuclear waste and the weapons industry

Some people believe that closed nuclear plants should be completely sealed in concrete in order to contain radioactive materials. Others question the wisdom of this approach. They say containment efforts have not worked well in another related area, the nuclear weapons industry.

Government plants that make nuclear weapons

also make a great deal of high-level radioactive waste. This waste is often in a liquid or semisolid form called sludge. Sludge and other types of radioactive waste that will remain dangerous for thousands of years have contaminated underground water and soil near many of the nation's nuclear weapons plants and at dumps used by these plants.

Waste from nuclear weapons plants

An underground waste dump near the Idaho National Engineering Laboratory near Idaho Falls is one example. The site was used like a garbage dump for contaminated wastes from a Colorado weapons manufacturing plant between the 1950s and 1970. "Some wastes were buried in steel barrels. But others . . . were dumped in wooden crates and cardboard boxes. The boxes and crates have long since decayed, and many of the steel barrels are now leaking," *The New York Times* reported in 1989.

The waste found at this site included gloves and aprons, which are considered low-level waste, and machinery considered to be in the middle range of radioactivity. Scientists say the three million cubic feet of buried waste found there has contaminated another five million cubic feet of soil.

Two plants, the Hanford Nuclear Reservation in Richland, Washington and the Savannah River Plant near Aiken, South Carolina, have generated nearly one hundred million gallons of highly radioactive wastes, *Time* magazine reported in 1988. "At Hanford alone," *Time*'s Ed Magnuson wrote, "some two hundred billion gallons of the more benign low-level wastes have been dumped into ponds, pits and basins—enough to create a lake forty feet deep and large enough to cover Manhattan."

The Hanford plant was closed in 1988, as were

several other nuclear weapons plants. Estimates for cleanup of the Hanford site alone run as high as $57 billion, the *Los Angeles Times* reported in 1990. Cleanup costs for all of the nation's nuclear weapons plants range from $91 billion over a thirty-year period to $200 billion over a sixty-year period.

In recent years, Hanford area residents learned that they may have been exposed to many forms of radioactive waste from the plant. Documents obtained by a Spokane, Washington, environmental group revealed that the Hanford plant released huge amounts of radioactive iodine into the air between 1944 and 1956. This information left residents badly shaken, but not surprised. Hanford area residents, who have nicknamed one area near town "death mile," claim they have suffered an unusually high number of cancer deaths and thyroid and other health problems because of

NUCLEAR WASTE COMPLEXES ACROSS THE U.S.

- Hanford Plant
- Idaho National Engineering Lab.
- Lawrence Livermore National Lab.
- Nevada Test Site
- Rocky Flats Plant
- Kansas City Plant
- Mound Plant
- Feed Materials Production Center
- Los Alamos National Laboratory
- Pantex Plant
- Sandia National Lab.
- Y-12 Plant
- Waste Isolation Pilot Plant
- Savannah River Plant
- Pinellas Plant

Source: United States Department of Energy; Nuclear Weapons Complex Modernization Report.

exposure to plant waste. The federal government is studying health problems reported by area residents.

Neighbors of another weapons plant, Feed Materials Production Center in Fernald, Ohio, made a similar discovery not long ago. The federal government recently admitted that it knew for decades that the Fernald plant had released tons of radioactive uranium wastes into the environment, exposing thousands of workers and residents to contamination. Ohio environmental officials also have estimated that the plant discharged 167,000 pounds of waste into the Great Miami River and that another 12.7 million pounds were placed in pits which may have been leaking.

The federal government also agreed to study

In New York, demonstrators carry anti-nuclear banners during a protest against nuclear power.

the problems around the Fernald plant. And, in 1990, a group of area residents won a seventy-eight million dollar lawsuit against the federal government in connection with waste emissions from the plant.

Nuclear waste from medical technology

A relatively small amount of low-level nuclear waste comes from the medical community. Radioactive materials are used to diagnose illnesses and treat diseases in hospitals all over the country. About 120 million medical procedures with radioactive materials are performed each year. Nuclear waste from these medical procedures consists of paper, syringes, needles, bottles, linens, and chemicals. In one year, an average-size hospital generates enough low-level nuclear waste to fill a large room.

At medical research facilities, nuclear materials help scientists develop new medicines. Animals are used in some experiments with radioactive materials. After the experiments are completed, their radioactive bodies are also considered low-level waste. Because some nuclear waste from medical procedures and research decays rapidly, it can be stored for a few days and then discarded with the regular trash. A few of these wastes retain their potency for decades and require disposal in trenches at a designated waste site.

The waste no one wants

The thought of storing nuclear waste in one's own community causes alarm. People imagine the devastation from the first atomic bomb and highly publicized nuclear power plant accidents. They worry about even small amounts of radiation that may escape from trenches. In the past, scientists suggested unrealistic solutions to nuclear waste disposal. They suggested that the waste be

launched into space, dumped into the oceans, or shipped to Antarctica. Some nuclear waste was dumped into the ocean, but that was stopped in the 1950s. Though still searching for an ideal disposal method, most nuclear waste is treated, placed in special containers, and buried in trenches.

In the late 1970s, six commercial sites existed for burying low-level nuclear waste. Leaks and other problems forced three of them to shut down. This meant that only three remaining sites were open to serve the entire country: Barnwell, South Carolina; Hanford, Washington; and Beatty, Nevada.

The governors of these states were unhappy about serving as the nation's dumping ground for nuclear waste. In protest, the governors of Nevada and Washington closed their sites in 1979. This meant that the small town of Barnwell, South Carolina, was receiving most of the country's low-level nuclear garbage. Governor Richard Riley of South Carolina responded forcefully. He declared that his state was not the "solution" to the country's nuclear waste problems.

With that proclamation, Riley reduced by one-half the amount of waste accepted at the Barnwell site. To further stir up the issue, he threatened to close the site altogether. This action forced Congress to look at the nation's nuclear waste disposal policies and to quickly respond to prevent a national disposal crisis.

Congress reacted to Riley's threat by passing

Nuclear workmen put on protective gear before entering a closed nuclear facility in California.

Governor Richard Riley of South Carolina threatened to close the nuclear dumping site in Barnwell, which was receiving most of the country's low-level waste. Congress reacted by passing the Low-level Waste Policy Act, which declares that states must dispose of their own low-level nuclear wastes.

the Low-level Radioactive Waste Policy Act in 1980. The law declares that states are responsible for their own low-level waste disposal. States must build disposal facilities individually or join together to share sites. States that do not build a facility or team up with others will be denied access to disposal facilities. States were not pleased by this move and failed to meet the first deadline in 1986. To give them extra time, Congress extended the deadline to 1996.

The majority of states have plans underway to handle their low-level nuclear wastes. Most states have teamed up with their neighbors to share disposal sites. A few states, such as Texas and New York, are building disposal facilities strictly for their own use.

Texas produces 130,000 cubic feet of low-level waste per year, enough to cover a football field three feet deep. About 80 percent of Texas's waste comes from four nuclear power plants. The remaining low-level nuclear waste comes from hospitals, universities, and industry. By 1991, Texas expects to have its own disposal site in operation. In the past, low-level waste produced there was shipped all the way to Hanford, Washington, for disposal.

Seeking other solutions

For the most part, nuclear waste has been stored temporarily in underground tanks or in pools of water near the reactors that created it. These methods have been less than successful. But scientists are searching for safer and more permanent storage and disposal methods for nuclear waste. This search focuses on two areas: ways to treat or package radioactive waste to make it less hazardous and where to put that waste once it is treated or packaged.

One idea for treating such waste uses a device

called a "gas plasma reactor." The reactor breaks down toxic chemicals using oxygen and intense heat. In the process, contaminated soil, toxic metals, and radioactive material melt inside the reactor into a hard glassy substance that can be more safely stored.

Another similar process, called "in situ vitrification," heats and melts contaminated soil still in the ground using high-voltage electricity. Radioactive machinery and barrels containing other radioactive waste would be fused into a glass-like substance right in the ground. This new substance could then be moved to a safer storage site.

Scientists are also experimenting with microorganisms that may help filter radioactive wastes

Scientists hope to fuse radioactive waste in glass logs that will be stored at the Savannah River plant in South Carolina.

from water. This process, like the others, will not get rid of hazardous waste. "Nothing like this can be made to go away," Patrick Dugan of the Idaho National Engineering Laboratory near Idaho Falls told *The New York Times* in 1989. "The hope is to find ways to move this material around so that it can be handled better."

Federal officials consider deep burial in a dry, stable, desolate area the safest way to permanently dispose of radioactive waste. The federal government has selected several possible burial sites, including Nevada's Yucca Mountain and a salt mine near Carlsbad, New Mexico.

At the New Mexico site, radioactive waste would be deposited 2,150 feet underground and then sealed with cement and compacted salt. Some geologists say the earth at that site is both stable and dry and therefore would make a good place for burial. But others have warned that the site stands over an underground reservoir.

Government geologists favor the Nevada site, which is located about one hundred miles northwest of Las Vegas. The dry, desert soil would bind up radioactive material and prevent it from traveling underground, they say. But some researchers have warned that the possibility of volcanic activity in the area could pose a problem.

Until an underground site is ready for use, federal officials plan to use a new billion-dollar complex near the Savannah River plant in South Carolina. There, in a honeycomb of concrete built underground, officials hope to store radioactive waste converted into glass logs ten feet long and two feet in diameter.

Finding solutions for safe disposal of radioactive waste still poses many problems. Scientists have a great deal of work to do in this area, as do their counterparts working on ways of reducing the dangers of other forms of hazardous waste.

Managing Hazardous Waste—Now and in the Future

TWO DECADES AGO, the hazardous waste "mess oozed its way into the nation's consciousness," *Time* magazine's Ed Magnuson wrote in 1985. At that time, hazardous waste management was a new science with much research yet to be done. Engineers, chemists, and scientists had to pool their skills to devise safer ways of handling waste.

Burying the problem

For several years, the EPA and researchers believed that better designed landfills, injection wells, surface impoundments, and incinerators were the answer to handling hazardous waste. One model landfill near Chicago was specially designed to safely contain waste.

This landfill covered two acres and was thirty-five feet deep. The bottom portion was lined with clay that extended another forty feet beneath the bottom of the hole. Several alternating layers of

(opposite page) A member of the National Campaign Against Toxic Hazards (NCATH) fills a barrel with letters to U.S. senators and congressmen. NCATH hopes to call attention to the problem of toxic waste dumping.

plastic liners and plastic grid systems were placed over the clay. If any waste or rainwater seeped below a certain point, it was collected in these liners and pumped out. Special tanks to receive the waste were made from concrete lined with epoxy, a gluelike substance that becomes very hard when it dries.

Landfills like the one near Chicago seemed to be a solution to the hazardous waste problem. And, some well-run landfills have provided an important option for dealing with hazardous waste. But hazardous waste was not so easily contained. When leaks appeared in even the most soundly constructed landfills, the government ordered a "land ban." This ban required companies to dump less waste in landfills and burn more of it in incinerators.

Is burning the answer?

Incinerators are specially designed ovens for burning large quantities of hazardous waste. Inside an incinerator, temperatures reach two thousand degrees Fahrenheit. Burning the waste tends to break down harmful substances into less toxic ones. Compounds containing carbon, called or-

Radioactive waste is unloaded for burial at a toxic dump site in Barnwell, South Carolina. Scientists are looking for other methods of handling waste, such as incineration.

ganic compounds, are best suited for disposal by incineration. This is because these chemicals break down more readily when exposed to heat and oxygen.

Some waste is resistant to the extreme temperatures of incineration. Heavy metals such as lead or cadmium may retain their toxic qualities despite burning. Sometimes, new and even more toxic chemicals, like dioxin, are created by the heating process. The EPA warns that these new chemicals "are more difficult to destroy and may be more toxic than the parent compound."

For the most part, incinerators can reduce quantities of hazardous waste. But they create another problem—air pollution. Incinerators release potentially harmful gases and ash into the air during the burning process.

In the town of Lenoir, North Carolina, residents have fought to stop pollution they contend has been caused by the Caldwell System incinerator. For more than ten years, residents have

A huge pile of ashes accumulates next to a waste incinerator in Philadelphia, Pennsylvania. Some scientists warn that the ash and gases created by incineration may be harmful.

complained to environmental officials that the incinerator causes health problems for them and their livestock. The EPA investigated the incinerator in response to citizen complaints. In its investigation, the EPA found that too much hazardous material was escaping from the plant. This led officials to wonder whether a similar problem might exist elsewhere. In an effort to find out, government officials ordered inspections of about two dozen of the nation's commercially operated waste incinerators.

The tide of public opinion continues to turn against incinerators. Stinging eyes, sinus infections, and strong odors have been reported by residents of Rock Hill, South Carolina. They blame ThermalKEM, the company that operates a local toxic waste incinerator, for these health problems. When the EPA inspected the incinerator, it found many operating problems that could cause toxic emissions to escape.

Toxic ash, produced by incinerators, at one time posed a serious environmental problem. In the past, this ash was deposited in unlined landfills, near wetlands, and even in parking lots. Most states now recognize the health threat of this ash and require burial in landfills with special liners and devices to protect against seepage.

Bacteria battle the waste problem

In the search for safe, economical ways to control hazardous waste, scientists have turned to bacteria. Bacteria have been used to treat sewage for nearly a century. They perform the same function when released into a toxic waste site—they eat and digest harmful materials. During this process, the waste is broken down into substances that are not toxic.

Bacteria have been used to help clean up Superfund sites and major oil spills. When the *Exxon*

A worker uses absorbent cloth to clean oil-slicked rocks after the Exxon Valdez *disaster in 1989. Other workers sprayed fertilizer on the beaches to speed the growth of bacteria. This naturally occurring bacteria helped in the cleanup by consuming oil deposits.*

Valdez, a large oil tanker, ran aground in 1989, oil covered miles of the Alaskan coastline. Naturally occurring bacteria on the beaches were sprayed with fertilizer to speed their growth. As they grew, they consumed oil deposits up to twelve inches below the surface.

The military is studying other uses for bacteria. At Tyndall Air Force Base in Florida, researchers are testing bacteria that eat toxins released by recycling missile fuel. The Air Force recycles more than 100 million gallons of rocket fuel to use for other purposes. In the recycling process the valuable chemicals in the fuel are separated and saved. Unfortunately, the leftover liquid is toxic. Researchers at the base are experimenting with organisms that eat the toxic chemicals and turn them into harmless materials.

Bacteria hold future promise for battling hazardous waste. They are inexpensive, and they destroy toxic substances instead of transferring them from one place to another.

Dumping on other countries

Even today, with strict laws controlling treatment and storage, waste management is a difficult problem. Proper disposal methods are expensive for businesses, and costs keep rising. For this reason, some businesses have found another way to deal with hazardous waste. They ship it to other countries.

The United States legally exports tons of hazardous waste, city garbage, and scrap metal to Canada, Mexico, Taiwan, Zimbabwe, and other nations. Exporting hazardous waste and potentially hazardous materials is a booming business with few legal restrictions. The exporter simply notifies the EPA about the shipment. If the government of the destination country agrees to accept it, the EPA can do little to stop the transaction.

Much of the waste goes to poor, undeveloped nations, sometimes called Third World countries. They are often eager to buy cheap chemical by-products found in the waste to use in their own manufacturing processes. Countries like Haiti allow waste to be deposited in their landfills for a fee. For the company exporting the waste, the fee is usually cheaper than disposal costs in the United States. For poor Third World nations, the benefit is acquiring desirable U.S. dollars.

The recycling of scrap metals, discarded electronics, and old batteries shipped from the Untied States has become big business. Despite the economic advantages, recycling without restrictions is hazardous. Many nations, especially less developed ones, have few laws controlling substances that pollute the land, air, and water. In Taiwan, for example, a local doctor reported in 1990 that he had found high lead levels in children attending a school located near a battery recycling plant. The students showed signs of lead poisoning, a condition that can cause severe brain and nerve damage. The school was forced to close.

Another example can be found in the People's Republic of China. As late as 1990, discarded electronics and other waste—some containing dangerous PCBs—were being tossed into a ravine located near a recycling plant. Eventually, this waste may taint the groundwater on which local villagers depend.

Should the U.S. put an end to global dumping?

Should the United States care about how other nations handle hazardous waste? Are exporters taking advantage of nations with few environmental laws? Some say the United States should put an end to global dumping. Exporting toxics has the potential to poison countless innocent people and damage precious natural resources. Shipping waste to other nations simply transfers the problem beyond our borders. The waste threatens people who are less knowledgeable about the risks and who are poorly prepared to deal with them.

In 1989, delegates from around the world met in Switzerland to attack the problem of global dumping. The majority of Third World nations wanted to outlaw hazardous waste exports. But the industrialized nations fought to continue exporting their dangerous cargo with only minor restrictions. One official at the EPA said that hazardous waste has become a serious foreign policy issue for the United States because a country's status in the world community is certain to diminish as long as it keeps sending discarded poisons to neighboring nations. Despite the risk of a bad image, industrialized nations continue to export

A large tanker carries a load of potentially hazardous sludge that will be dumped in the North Sea.

This abandoned waste site is filled with toxic chemicals that may be seeping into the soil and polluting groundwater. Many environmentalists believe that minimizing waste is more efficient than storing it once it exists.

their waste because it is such a cheap and easy solution.

The difficulties of dealing with hazardous waste have led some people to conclude that creating less waste may be more efficient than searching for ways of getting rid of it once it exists. "The real solution to the toxic crisis is to prevent pollution at its source," says the environmen-

tal group Greenpeace. This method of minimizing waste is called source reduction.

The federal government agrees with this approach. A 1990 EPA report states that "the preferred manner of managing waste is not to generate it in the first place." Though the idea of generating less waste has great possibilities, only a few companies have made it work.

The Minnesota Mining & Manufacturing Company (3M) has taken source reduction seriously. This company produces tape and other adhesives. By switching from a toxic, solvent-based glue to a water-based glue, the company has slashed hazardous waste production by nearly half. Chemical companies, such as Monsanto and Dow, have also made strides in reducing waste or recycling it. "We are now generating less and recycling more," Monsanto's Larry O'Neil said.

Producing less waste

General Dynamics, based in St. Louis, is another company that has drastically reduced toxic waste. This company makes jets, submarines, tanks, and missiles for the military. In just four years, General Dynamics invested thirty-six million dollars in waste reduction and eliminated forty million pounds of waste. Ultimately, the company hopes to produce no hazardous waste. How did all of this happen? It began with a sincere commitment by top-level managers. The company's former president, Oliver C. Boileau, explained his philosophy. "All employees of this company, international as well as domestic, have a responsibility to protect the environment."

To produce less waste, General Dynamics used several different techniques. Where possible, less toxic chemicals were substituted for the dangerous ones. In another move, all single-walled underground storage tanks were either replaced with double-walled tanks or installed with leak-detection devices. In some of the manufacturing processes, General Dynamics developed ways to recover metals and reuse or sell them to other companies. The success of these efforts has made General Dynamics a model for industry. Some companies refuse to share waste reduction technology secrets. But General Dynamics wants other companies to know what it has achieved and how. "We are proud of our accomplishments and are happy to tell them," commented one of the company's environmental managers.

Even small businesses can reduce their toxic waste output. Jeff Shumay owns an auto repair shop in McLean, Virginia. Instead of dumping used oil and antifreeze down the drain or into the ground as most shops do, he recycles them. The recycling machine cleanses old antifreeze so it can be used again. Used oil serves as the fuel to operate the antifreeze recycler.

The recycling machine was expensive, but converting to environmentally safe technology has paid off. Shumay says his business has increased because customers know he is protecting the environment.

Citizens must help

Individuals also have a responsibility to remove toxic waste from their own homes and dispose of it safely.

Small amounts of potentially toxic waste can be found in most homes. Old buckets of paint, used oil, and cleaning products create problems when pitched into landfills with regular garbage. The toxic chemicals in household products can leak into groundwater, cause fires, or explode. To prevent household toxic waste from reaching trash landfills or being dumped in someone's backyard, some communities have set up a special program

In Arlington, Virginia, citizen groups from around the country demonstrate against toxic waste dumping. Besides rallying against unsafe industrial practices, individuals can help the waste problem by safely disposing of toxic waste in their own homes.

to collect the waste. This program is called Amnesty Days. The word *amnesty* means to grant forgiveness or pardon. During Amnesty Days, citizens can turn in their toxic materials for safe disposal without having to pay a fee. In one community in Florida, residents turned in over seventy-two thousand pounds of toxic waste during Amnesty Days. Of that amount, thirty-eight thousand pounds, over half, was recyclable.

Americans can help in other ways as well. Changing buying habits by purchasing fewer products that pollute is one way. "The high standard of living Americans enjoy depends on an abundance of manufactured products—and with those products come hazardous by-products," explains author Irene Kiefer. If Americans learn to depend less on products that produce hazardous waste, industry might then follow that example by coming up with nonhazardous products and technologies.

What next?

Recovering from decades of environmental abuse is not easy. A great deal of work must be done. Though progress has been painfully slow, the world must move forward with new ideas and a stronger commitment. For when we pollute the

"I think we're making progress . . . They printed their latest incineration proposal on recycled paper."

environment, we also pollute ourselves and the things we need to survive.

People of all ages and backgrounds need to get involved. One place to start is by writing or calling elected government officials. Often lawmakers do not hear from the people they represent. Citizens must make their desires known to elected officials, leaders of industry, and to people who have the power to change the way society operates.

Careful and considerate treatment of the planet will ensure not only our own well-being but that of future generations. Working together and as individuals, we can still develop solutions to the problem of what to do with too much waste.

Glossary

compound: A substance made up of two or more elements.

curies: A measurement of the amount of radioactivity emitted.

dioxin: A family of chemicals, some of which can be very toxic. Dioxin is used as an herbicide, is produced as a toxic waste by-product of paper bleaching, and is released when paper or plastics are burned.

gas plasma reactor: A device that uses oxygen and intense heat to break down toxic chemicals in contaminated materials and waste.

groundwater: Underground water that supplies wells and springs. As it trickles downward, the water fills spaces in rocks. About half of the population of the United States relies on groundwater as its source of drinking water.

herbicide: A substance used to control or eliminate weeds.

incineration: The burning of hazardous waste at extremely high temperatures.

in situ vitrification: A process that uses intense heat to melt contaminated soil and materials still in the ground; breaks down hazardous substances.

landfill: A large pit in the ground where waste or trash is buried. Layers of refuse are covered with soil as the landfill slowly builds up.

leachate: Liquid that has penetrated hazardous waste primarily in a landfill and creates a leaking stream of the harmful substances.

mercury: A metal used in various manufacturing processes. Inhaling mercury vapors or ingesting food, such as fish, laced with mercury can cause nervous disorders and even death.

nuclear waste: Hazardous waste that is radioactive.

PCB: Polychlorinated biphenyls; a dangerous chemical originally used as liquid insulation in electrical products. PCBs were banned in 1979 in the U.S.

pesticide: A substance used to kill or control insects or rodents.

radioactive: The condition of something that has been exposed to radiation. Radiation is energy emitted from atoms in the form of particles or waves; it can damage or destroy living cells.

solvent: A substance, usually a liquid, that can dissolve another substance. Dry cleaners use solvents to remove dirt from clothing.

Superfund: A popular name given to a federal law that created a list of dangerous hazardous waste sites.

surface impoundment: A pit or area surrounded by embankments.

tailings: A sandlike substance that is a by-product of the process that separates uranium ore from the rock and dirt in which it is encased. Tailings are radioactive and potentially dangerous.

toxic: Poisonous.

Organizations to Contact

The following organizations are concerned with the issues covered in this book. All of them have publications or information available for interested readers.

Chemical Manufacturers Association
2501 M St. NW
Washington, DC 20037

Citizens Clearinghouse for Hazardous Waste
PO Box 926
Arlington, VA 22216

Department of Health and Human Services
Public Health Center
Centers for Disease Control
Atlanta, GA 30333

Environmental and Occupational Health Sciences Institute
45 Knightsbridge Rd.
Brookwood Plaza II
Piscataway, NJ 08854-3923

Environmental Protection Agency
Public Information Center
401 M St. SW
Washington, DC 20460

Greenpeace USA
1436 U St. NW
Washington, DC 20009

Radioactive Waste Campaign
625 Broadway
Second Floor
New York, NY 10012

The Sierra Club
730 Polk St.
San Francisco, CA 94109

Suggestions for Further Reading

Margaret and Bruce Hyde, *Everyone's Trash Problem: Nuclear Wastes*. New York: McGraw-Hill, 1979.

Irene Kiefer, *Poisoned Land*. New York: Atheneum, 1981.

Ed Magnuson, "They Lied to Us," *Time*, October 31, 1988.

David Newton, *Taking a Stand Against Environmental Pollution*. New York: Franklin Watts, 1990.

Anne Underwood, "The Return to Love Canal," *Newsweek*, July 30, 1990.

Malcolm Weiss, *Toxic Waste*. New York: Franklin Watts, 1984.

Stephen Zipko, *Toxic Threat*. New York: Julian Messner, 1986.

Works Consulted

Rudy Abramson, "A Nuclear Drama Is Brewing," *Los Angeles Times*, November 18, 1990.

Associated Press, "Residents Angry About Dumping," *Charleston (SC) News and Courier*, July 28, 1990.

Bruce Biewald and Donald Marron, "Nuclear Power Economics: Construction, Operation, and Disposal," *Science for the People*, May/June 1989.

Michael Brown, *Laying Waste*. New York: Washington Square Press, 1981.

Charles Campbell, "People Want to Do the Right Thing," *Panama City (FL) News Herald,* November 5, 1990.

Chemecology, "A Tiny Solution to a Big Problem," September 1990.

Chemecology, "Public Opinion and Science Set Separate Agendas for EPA," November 1990.

Clement Associates, *Toxicological Profile for Mercury*. Washington, DC: Agency for Toxic Substances and Disease Registry, 1989.

Barry Commoner, *Making Peace with the Planet*. New York: Pantheon Books, 1990.

Paula DiPerna, *Cluster Mystery*. New York: C.V. Mosby, 1985.

Michael R. Edelstein, *Contaminated Communities*. Boulder, CO: Westview Press, 1988.

The EPA Journal, "Superfund: Looking Back, Looking Ahead," December 1987.

Prentiss Findlay, "Agencies Target S.C. Incinerator," *Charleston (SC) News and Courier*, August 1, 1990.

Reed Glenn, "Used Oil Compels Recycling," *Panama City (FL) News Herald*, October 13, 1990.

Michael Gochfeld, *INFOsheet—Superfund: Hazardous Waste Clean Up*. Piscataway, NJ: Environmental and Occupational Health Sciences Institute, 1989.

Greenpeace USA, "Hazardous Waste Incinerators," Washington, DC, 1987.

Greenpeace USA, "Industry, the Environmental Crisis, and Greenwashing," Washington, DC, 1990.

Stephen Higgins, "TAFB Tests 'Bugs' That Eat Missile Toxins," *Panama City (FL) News Herald*, July 22, 1990.

League of Women Voters Education Fund, *The Nuclear Waste Primer*. New York: Nick Lyons Books, 1985.

Robert E. Long, ed., *The Problem of Waste Disposal*. New York: H.W. Wilson, 1989.

Jon R. Luoma, "U.S. Turning to New Technologies to Clean Up Arms Plants," *The New York Times*, January 3, 1989.

Pollution Engineering, "General Dynamics Eliminates 40 Million Pounds of Hazardous Waste in 4 Years," May 1989.

Joyce Pugh, "Elevated Dioxin Levels Prompt HRS Warnings," *Panama City (FL) News Herald*, September 22, 1990.

George D. Russ Jr., *Low Level Radioactive Waste: Building a Perspective*. Bethesda, MD: Atomic Industrial Forum, 1986.

Heidi Schultz, *Solving the Hazardous Waste Problem*. Washington, DC: U.S. Environmental Protection Agency, 1986.

Syracuse Research Corporation, *Toxicological Profile for 2, 3, 7, 8-Tetrachlorodibenzo-p-Dioxin*. Washington, DC: Agency for Toxic Substances and Disease Registry, 1989.

Toxic Times, "Turning the Wastes of War into a War on Waste," Summer 1990.

U.S. Environmental Protection Agency, *An Analysis of State Superfund Programs: 50-State Study*. Washington, DC: Government Printing Office, 1989.

U.S. Environmental Protection Agency, "Hazardous Wastes," *Environmental Backgrounder*, January 1989.

U.S. Environmental Protection Agency, *RCRA Orientation Manual*. Washington, DC: Government Printing Office, 1990.

Matthew L. Wald, "Finding a Burial Place for Nuclear Wastes Grows More Difficult," *The New York Times*, December 5, 1989.

Daniel J. Watts, *INFOsheet—Waste Reduction*. Piscataway, NJ: Environmental and Occupational Health Sciences Institute, 1989.

Index

About the Author

Lila Gano is the author of two other nonfiction books published by Lucent Books, *Smoking* and *Television: Electronic Pictures*. Ms. Gano started her career after college as a naval officer and served in San Diego, California, and Hawaii. While in the Navy, she obtained a master's degree in psychology. As a civilian, she has worked in the defense industry as a technical writer and project manager. Her home is in Panama City, Florida, where she lives with her husband, Rich.

Ms. Gano is a member of the Society of Children's Book Writers and is the publicity director for the Panhandle Writers' Guild in Florida. She enjoys traveling and racquetball and is working on her first screenplay.

Picture Credits

Photos supplied by Research Plus, Mill Valley, California

Cover photo by David M. Doody/Uniphoto Picture Agency
AP/Wide World Photos, 8, 10, 13, 17, 27, 32, 40, 42, 52, 54,
   57, 58, 65, 72, 75
Department of Energy, 67
Environmental Protection Agency, 6, 23, 28, 78
Greenpeace, 73, 77
H. Frost, F.P.G., 30
United Nations, 39
United Nations/R. Ericson, 34
UPI/Bettmann Newsphotos, 12, 15, 16, 19, 20, 25, 26, 46,
   49, 50, 62, 66, 70, 81
Vermont Travel Division, 36
The Weyerhaeuser Co., 33